Edith Rigby
Library & Learning Centre
Tel: 01772 225298

PRESTON
COLLEGE

Please return or renew on or before the date shown below.
Fines will be charged on overdue items.

– 1 NOV 2005	1 4 DEC 2007	
1 5 FEB 2006	2 9 APR 2014	
– 8 MAR 2010	2007	
2 0 APR 2010		
– 5 MAY 2011		
2 4 APR 2014		

Class 796.077 CRI

Barcode 081059

ysing
our
Coaching

© The National Coaching Foundation, 2005

Reprinted 2003 © **sports coach UK**

First published 1998 © The National Coaching Foundation

This resource is copyright under the Berne Convention. All rights are reserved. Apart from any fair dealing for the purposes of private study, criticism or review, as permitted under the Copyright, Designs and Patents Act 1988, no part of this publication can be reproduced, stored in a retrieval system, or transmitted in any form or by any means, electronic, electrical, chemical, mechanical, optical, photocopying, recording or otherwise, without the prior written permission of the copyright owner. Enquiries should be addressed to **Coachwise Business Solutions**.

sports coach UK is the brand name of The National Coaching Foundation and has been such since April 2001

ISBN-13: 978-1-902523-14-8
ISBN-10: 1-902523-14-8

Author: Penny Crisfield

Editors: Phil Cabral and Andy Miles

Sub-editors: Frank Herold and Bill Galvin

Typesetter: Debbie Backhouse

sports coach UK would like to thank Auriel Forrester and Ian Moir for reviewing the resource.

Cover photo courtesy of
sportscotland/Glasgow City Council

Published on behalf of
sports coach UK by

sports coach UK
114 Cardigan Road
Headingley
Leeds LS6 3BJ
Tel: 0113-274 4802 Fax: 0113-275 5019
Email: coaching@sportscoachuk.org
Website: www.sportscoachuk.org

Patron: HRH The Princess Royal

Coachwise Business Solutions
Coachwise Ltd
Chelsea Close
Off Amberley Road
Armley
Leeds LS12 4HP
Tel: 0113-231 1310 Fax: 0113-231 9606
Email: enquiries@coachwisesolutions.co.uk
Website: www.coachwisesolutions.co.uk

040278

How do you become a better coach? Most coaches work hard to improve their athlete's performance but few make the same level of commitment towards their coaching development. Coaching is both an art and a science which requires extensive knowledge, skills and experience to help performers develop their potential physically, emotionally and socially as well as technically and tactically. In order to become a better or more *effective* coach, you must decide where you are, where you want to end up and how you are going to get there.

This resource will help you identify the coach you want to become. Working through it, you will analyse your coaching and pinpoint the developments you will make to improve your coaching practice. The resource will help you take responsibility for your ongoing improvement as a coach through a process of analysis based on critical thinking, and continuous self-evaluation and reflection. The foundation of this self-improvement process is your desire to learn more and willingness to change in the pursuit of personal excellence.

While this resource will provide you with a process for analysing and developing your coaching, it cannot provide the level of help and feedback available at the associated **sports coach UK (scUK)** workshop[1]. The workshop outlines the process of self-analysis, evaluation and reflection in greater detail and gives you the opportunity to discuss and share your experiences with other coaches[2]. The material in this resource will build on your workshop experiences and help you relate them to your practice. If you have not attended the workshop, you should work through the resource methodically.

Whether or not you have attended the workshop, this resource will show you how to reflect on your coaching practice through the use of videos, diaries, peer coaches and mentors. It will help you identify your goals, clarify your beliefs, analyse your strengths and weaknesses and determine ways to develop your coaching skills, knowledge and experience. By the end of the resource, you will have learned the core analytical skills and will have worked through a process for evaluating and improving your coaching.

No short cut exists to becoming an effective coach – this resource is just *the start of your journey towards coaching excellence.* The direction in which you travel and how far you go will depend on your vision and desire to become an effective coach. The ideal coach does not exist so you must take responsibility for determining your coaching effectiveness. Decision-making is an integral part of coaching and the decisions you make will determine your effectiveness. They will be influenced by your goals, beliefs, knowledge, skill, experience and roles. These factors are all within your control and you can change them to become a more effective coach. Regular self-analysis through the process outlined in this resource will help you gauge your progress and ensure you stay on your path to coaching excellence.

---

1   For further details of **scUK** workshops in your area, contact the **scUK** Business Support Centre (BSC), Tel: 01509-226130, Email: bsc@sportscoachuk.org

2   It is assumed that coaches working through this resource will have sufficient coaching experience on which to draw – for example as a minimum, those qualified at Level Two and working towards Level Three, or those working regularly with good club level performers. The workshop will also offer useful insights for coaches with greater experience (even those working in the high performance area).

Throughout this resource, the pronouns he, she, him, her and so on are interchangeable and intended to be inclusive of both males and females. It is important in sport, as elsewhere, that both genders have equal status and opportunities.

Contents

CHAPTER ONE:
Introduction

Effective coaches develop people – they help to make them better performers and more rounded and capable people who can work well with others, and identify and achieve their goals in sport and life. Effective coaching is therefore more than it might seem at first, for it involves developing the whole person – physically, technically, tactically, emotionally and socially.

Effective coaches need knowledge about the sport, and they need the skills and experience to help performers achieve their goals. The way coaches attain this knowledge, skill and experience will vary. What it means, however, is that coach training is not just a quick fix gained by attending courses and gaining qualifications. These courses and qualifications are, of course, invaluable for improving knowledge and technical skills. However, effective coaches also build on the things they do well and learn from their mistakes and advice from other people. These coaches are willing to examine their performance in the light of their experiences and seek out others

> Good coaches seek constant improvement in their search for personal coaching excellence – they have an open mind and an insatiable thirst for knowledge; they have a strong and innovative capacity to develop and execute their skills within an ethical framework in which the performer's respect and welfare is paramount.

to help them in this process. This resource will take you through a systematic analytical process to help you improve your effectiveness.

> - Successful coaches love what they do, their job is their passion.
> - Expert coaching is hard work combined with day-to-day learning (Moraes, 1996[1]).

The Decision-making Process

Decision-making is a fundamental part of coaching. Coaches continually make decisions about what to do (the action to carry out in a particular situation) and how to do it (the way to carry it out or their behaviour). Their knowledge, skill and experience influence their decisions along with their:

- perception of the situation, the conditions, the performers and their goals

- current emotional state (eg happy, nervous, pressured, frustrated)

- philosophy and beliefs

- personal coaching goals (ie their goals towards coaching effectiveness – see Figure 1).

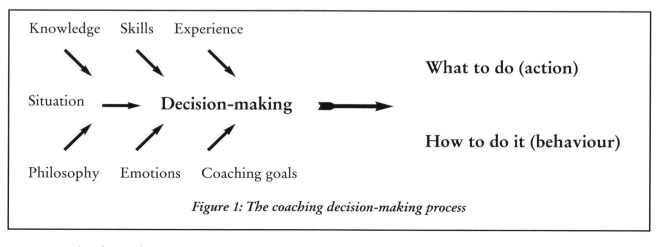

Figure 1: The coaching decision-making process

---

1   Extract taken from Salmela, J H (1996) **Great job coach**. Potentium, Ottawa. ISBN 0 9680935 0 7.

The decisions you make and your subsequent effectiveness are based on the interaction between these factors. Your goals and those of your performers determine the overall direction of your coaching; your choice of action is influenced by the situation, your knowledge, skill and experience; your behaviour is influenced by your philosophy (or underlying beliefs) and current emotional state. By examining your coaching experiences, reviewing your behaviour and questioning your actions (the reason why you did what you did, the other choices available and the consequences of these choices), you can learn from past decisions and plan or respond to future situations more effectively. Chapter Two will take you through this process.

Analysing your Decisions and Actions

This resource is based on the premise that to improve your coaching you should analyse and reflect on your decisions and subsequent actions. This entails examining all the factors that influence your decisions and, where appropriate, changing them to improve your future effectiveness. For example, you may feel you require greater knowledge, skills or experience to cope with a particular issue; you might recognise that your emotional state affects your behaviour in particular situations and is, therefore, not compatible with your underlying beliefs and philosophy; you might feel you need to find out more about your performers because you fail to consider each performer's specific needs and goals in the activities you set.

Few coaches have the luxury of a personal coach trainer or mentor to guide their experiences and provide feedback on their performance. The majority of coaches are rarely observed in practice and even when this does occur, more often than not they do not seek or receive much feedback. Although performers can give coaches valuable information, few coaches actively seek this information – perhaps because they are focusing on the performers and not their own performance. If you wish to improve your coaching effectiveness and do not have the luxury of a personal coach or mentor, you should undertake a process of self-analysis similar to the one outlined in this resource.

Enhancing Effectiveness

Having identified the particular factor or factors you wish to address, you can carry out specific tasks to enhance your effectiveness. For example:

- reading relevant information or observing other coaches to gain more knowledge
- attending workshops to develop your skills
- working with different performers to extend your experience
- spending more time with your performers to learn more about them
- examining your thoughts to manage your emotions better
- reviewing your decisions, actions and behaviour to ensure it is in line with your philosophy.

The underlying rationale for this resource and the accompanying workshop is that coaching is a lifelong process of personal development in which coaches not only seek excellence for their performers (if that is what each performer wants) but also for themselves. They seek to examine their coaching goals and philosophy, extend their knowledge and experience, and hone their skills in pursuit of their goals. This resource will, therefore, help you analyse your coaching performance to become a more effective coach.

On completion of this resource, you should be able to:

- analyse your coaching using video, checklists, diaries and live observation
- capitalise on external input (eg peer coaches, performers and mentors) to enhance your self-analysis and reflection
- examine your goals and philosophy
- explain your coaching decisions and subsequent actions and identify any discrepancies between them and your coaching goals and philosophy
- identify any changes you wish to make to enhance your coaching effectiveness
- devise and implement an action plan to modify your coaching in line with these changes.

Remember, there is no short cut to becoming a more effective coach – this resource is just the start of a journey towards coaching excellence. Which way you travel and how far you go will depend on your vision and desire to become a more effective coach. The first step on this journey is knowing the process for analysing your performance so you can put it into action. Chapter Two outlines this process.

CHAPTER TWO:
A Process to Analyse Coaching Performance

Analysing an athlete's performance is an integral part of most coaching sessions. You may, for example, analyse technique, commitment and teamwork or the performers' ability to handle pressure, retain concentration or cope with mistakes. The process involves observing and evaluating the effectiveness of each performance. Through this analysis, you are helping performers learn or improve.

Stop to think how you analyse their performance to help your athletes achieve their goals, learn new techniques or modify their behaviour.

ACTIVITY 1

Describe the process you use to help your athletes improve their performance (eg of a specific technique or of their performance in a competition):

You have probably described a systematic process in which you analyse the performer's behaviour, compare it with the desired behaviour, identify how to change or develop it, action plan to make that change, implement that plan and review progress (re-analyse) regularly. This change may require a physical change in technique, a social change in the way they interact with other performers or officials, emotional changes in their attitude or control, or cognitive (thought processing) changes in the way they interpret information and make decisions.

The process you described may look something like Figure 2, although you may have used different words. This is a typical process that coaches go through when analysing an athlete's performance. Often they go through this process unconsciously.

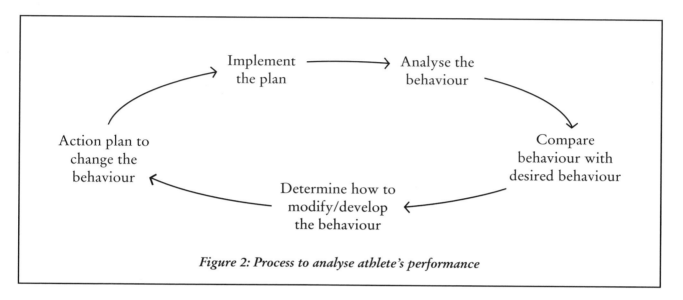

Figure 2: Process to analyse athlete's performance

You can analyse and improve your coaching performance by adopting a similar process (Figure 3).

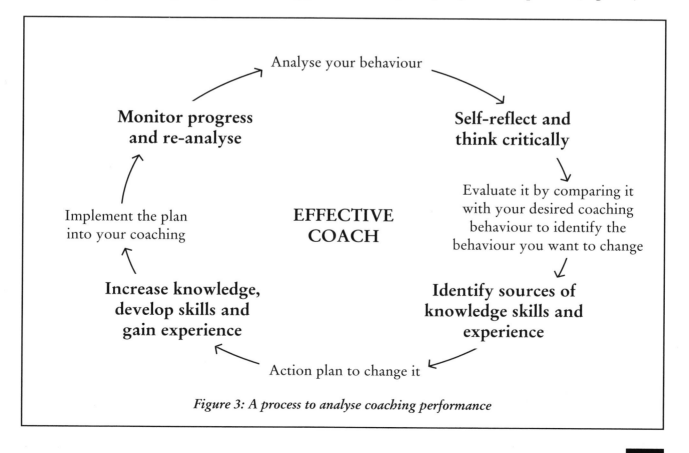

Figure 3: A process to analyse coaching performance

Improving your coaching effectiveness will take time. You would not expect to handle a phobia about spiders or learn a new sport technique instantly; you know you will need to invest considerable practice time and effort to achieve a lasting change. You may experience rapid improvement at certain times and plateaus when there are few, if any, noticeable gains. Even babies who are very receptive to learning take time to learn to walk – they make thousands of attempts and experience many failures before finally grasping the skill.

Adopting the Process

Changing your established response to typical situations can be more difficult than learning a new skill or reviewing your actions and behaviour in new situations. When your responses become habitual, usually when you experience a situation several times, you no longer tend to assess the situation consciously or with as much detail as you did when you initially experienced the situation. You may not consider the full range of options before deciding on your action. You may act and not review the outcome of your actions very thoroughly unless something unusual results. In a new situation, however, you have the opportunity to consider the situation from multiple perspectives and appraise all the factors before making a decision and responding (see Figure 1). This enables you to make the best decision for all concerned in that situation.

It is not always easy or appropriate to think through every situation or action. However, the challenge of effective coaching is to examine your perceptions and the factors that influence your decisions regularly, so you challenge your performers continually and help them improve consistently. Adopting this approach enables you to remain effective but requires you to analyse yourself and strive to improve so you continually challenge your performers. This is based on a cyclical process of continuous analysis, assessment and improvement for both you and your performers (see Figure 3).

Now you understand the process, the next step is to decide what kind of coach you want to become. The ideal coach does not exist but sport has many good coaches. You must decide for yourself how you would like to coach and having gained your vision, you should determine your goals for your coaching.

Once you have determined your goals, you need to become more aware of your behaviour generally and in specific situations – examine what you do, what you say and how you say it, and why you choose to act the way you do. This analysis is complicated by the fact that the way you coach may need to be different in different situations. You can compare this behaviour with your desired behaviour – that of the kind of coach you want to become. This comparison will help you identify what you need to do to move your current coaching behaviour closer to your ideal coaching behaviour. Action planning and goal-setting to implement the change takes further time and commitment. Finally you should re-analyse your coaching to monitor progress against the goals that you have set. The next few chapters will take you through this whole process in greater detail (see Figure 3); you will start by examining your thoughts on effective coaching.

CHAPTER THREE:
What is Effective Coaching?

What is coaching? What does it mean to you?

ACTIVITY 2

Stop to think what coaching really means to you by completing the following statements:

- Coaching is ...

- I coach because ...

- My goals as a coach are to ...

- The reason my performers take part is to ...

- To coach effectively I need ...

Coaching means different things to different people. For some, it is about providing enjoyable experiences through sport; for others it is about developing specific sport skills; for you it might be about competing and winning. Perhaps coaching is a way to help people achieve success and so develop important life skills such as self-confidence and control, mental toughness and commitment. It may be a combination of these things and indeed much more. People generally agree that coaches set exercises, practices and tasks to accelerate skill learning and produce improvements in performance. More experienced and enlightened coaches realise they also have a responsibility towards the social, emotional, physical and moral development of their performers. They coach people through sport rather than coaching the sport to people.

Effective coaches need knowledge ...

To help performers develop in these ways, coaches need to learn from a wide range of experiences, develop appropriate skills and apply their knowledge effectively.

Coaches need **knowledge** about:

- the technicalities and rules of their sport, the associated strategies and tactics, the competitive structures

- training principles and fitness strategies, how to design fitness sessions and programmes, how to test fitness and modify programmes according to the competitive year

- how people learn, execute, refine and maintain skills; how they can become more consistent and capable of successful execution in pressure situations

- how to plan and structure coaching sessions for maximum enjoyment and improvement; how to organise groups and ensure safety, and how to handle the administration

- how to strengthen the mental factors such as concentration and confidence that influence performance

- their performers – their goals, experiences, likes and dislikes, life outside sport, as well as their chronological, developmental and training age[1] if they are young people.

... skills and experience

Coaching knowledge on its own is of little value unless you can apply it to your coaching practice and use it to help your performers improve. You need a number of **skills** such as interpersonal skills, planning, problem-solving and teaching skills. In addition, good coaches need the personal skills of self-analysis and reflection to ensure they continue to develop their coaching effectiveness (see Chapter Five, page 17). Coaches can develop these skills through varied and quality **experience** but only if they use these opportunities to reflect on what they are doing, why and how effectively they are doing them. This is where the process of critical self-analysis and reflection is important to every coach's continuing development and effectiveness.

... a philosophy

Your coaching is strongly influenced by your coaching **philosophy.** This is about your aims and values, why you coach, and how you believe coaching benefits people. It embraces a set of personal and ethical guidelines which govern your behaviour as a coach. Such a philosophy is based on your beliefs about issues such as:

- your role in relation to performers and others such as the parents, other coaches, medical support staff, officials and administrators

- the extent to which your performers are responsible for their behaviour and development and identify their goals and contribute to the design of their training programmes

- the relative importance of the outcome of competition in relation to the long-term development and well-being of performers

- the importance of adhering to the rules, the meaning of fair play and the use of banned substances to increase performance

- the intensity of training and competition for children and young performers

- the need for single-minded commitment or the importance of balance in the performers' lives.

---

1   Children's chronological age (their actual age in years) may differ significantly from their developmental age (ie the extent to which their emotional, physical or social development compares, exceeds or falls short of that of a typical child of that age). The training age refers to the number of years the child may have been engaged in a specialised training programme. These terms are further examined in the **scUK** resource, *Coaching Young Performers*, available from **Coachwise 1st4sport** (tel 0113-201 5555 or visit www.1st4sport.com).

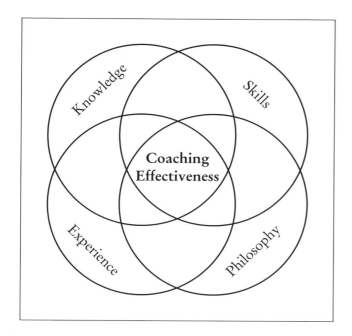

Coaching Effectiveness

Knowledge — Skills — Experience — Philosophy

Reflecting on what coaching means to you and why you do it is important because this information will give valuable insights into your coaching – how you coach now and how you would like to coach in the future. For example, some coaches are totally focused on winning; others may aim to encourage athletes to participate for fun, education or to develop healthy lifestyles. You need to focus on your coaching goals and philosophy and examine your behaviour to determine what sort of coach you want to become – in other words to determine precisely where you are heading in your quest to become a more effective coach. You may also want to check whether your coaching reflects your philosophy. Are your aims and values apparent in the way you coach?

You may not have thought about your philosophy and beliefs (or values) – usually you develop them as you interact with people, extend your knowledge and gain wide ranging experiences through life. Your philosophy and beliefs will affect your decisions and subsequent effectiveness. Therefore examining them is important. The next activity will help raise your awareness of their effects on your decisions and behaviour.

ACTIVITY 3

Your personal philosophy is based on your core values, the things you really believe in. Stop to think about your values as a coach and then write down up to five core values in the spaces below. If this proves quite difficult, use the following list to trigger your thoughts:

Honesty	Fairness	Empathy	Duty	Excellence	Personal responsibility
Commitment	Teamwork	Inclusion	Caring	Conformity	Freedom of choice
Loyalty	Physical fitness	Integrity	Challenge	Respect	Lifelong learning
Accountability	Self-discipline	Effort	Health	Success	Support

	Do not match at all				*Match fully*
_____	1	2	3	4	5
_____	1	2	3	4	5
_____	1	2	3	4	5
_____	1	2	3	4	5
_____	1	2	3	4	5

For each value you select, rate how well your coaching actions/behaviour match your beliefs on the five point scale.

Every coach will possess different knowledge, skills, experiences and will select different values in this activity. These differences ensure that no two coaches are the same. The decisions they make will be different or will be for different reasons. There is, therefore, no such thing as an ideal coach. However, there are many ways to become a more effective coach. These vary according to the needs and personality of each performer, as well as the values, knowledge, skills and experience of each coach. The important issue for you is to determine the type of coach you want to be and then take greater responsibility for deciding what you want to change or develop (ie your knowledge, skill, experience, goals and philosophy) to improve your effectiveness and take you closer to the type of coach you want to become.

The responsibilities and tasks you accept as a coach directly affect your decisions and the actions you take to implement those decisions. The next chapter helps you identify and reflect on your responsibilities, tasks and subsequent behaviours to see how they affect your coaching effectiveness and to see which areas, if any, you can or wish to change.

CHAPTER FOUR:
Coaching Responsibilities, Tasks and Behaviours

Core coaching responsibilities:

- Design and manage the programme or activity.
- Guide the athletes in training.
- Advise the athletes in competition.
- Support the athletes in their emotional response to training and competition.

Certain common coaching responsibilities exist, whatever your coaching goals and philosophy – designing the coaching programme, running the training session and supporting the performers in competition, for example. To meet these responsibilities, you will have to undertake specific tasks such as teaching techniques, providing feedback and planning competitions. Some tasks are undertaken away from the immediate coaching environment (with or without the performers), while others take place during the session or at the competitive event.

These tasks govern **what** you do, but **how** you choose to do them (your behaviour) determines your effectiveness. You need certain skills, knowledge and experience to undertake these tasks effectively[1]. Common coaching tasks include:

- analysing performance critically
- problem-solving and making ethically-sound decisions
- devising and implementing (or managing) a plan
- communicating (giving and receiving information, support, guidance)
- reviewing (evaluating) progress.

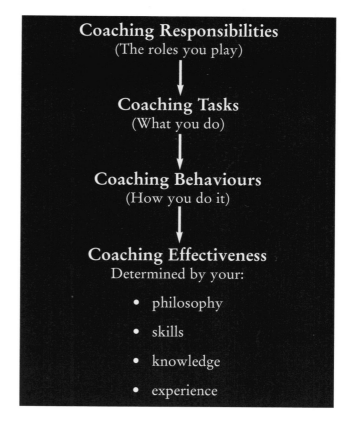

Coaching Responsibilities
(The roles you play)

↓

Coaching Tasks
(What you do)

↓

Coaching Behaviours
(How you do it)

↓

Coaching Effectiveness
Determined by your:

- philosophy
- skills
- knowledge
- experience

---

1   The term **competence** is frequently used in coach education as a benchmark or minimum standard. It refers to the coaches' capacity to use their skills, knowledge and experience to assess the needs of the performer in a specific context and provide effective guidance and support within an ethical framework.

For example, to fulfil your responsibility to instruct or train performers, you may decide to teach a new or develop an existing technique (eg a twisted somersault in gymnastics, trapping the ball in football). To carry out this task, you will draw, probably unconsciously, on your:

- **coaching philosophy** in the way you relate to the performers, introduce and run the practices, and in your expectations
- **goals** and those of your athletes in establishing the overall direction of the coaching and specific aims for each coaching session
- **skill** in analysing the action to establish its effectiveness, in determining what feedback to offer, and in communicating your thoughts to the athletes
- **knowledge** of the specific sport techniques, of how skills are learnt and developed, and of each athlete
- **experience** of particular issues, events and situations.

The interaction between these factors will influence your decisions and choice of action. Look at the following examples:

Decision 1

You might decide to set up a demonstration and explain the key points; you might decide to shout instructions and comments while they practise; you may place the performer physically in the desired position.

Decision 2

You can display enthusiasm or disinterest, pleasure or disappointment by the words you use or the non-verbal messages you send – consciously or unconsciously.

Decision 3

You might manage the practice very rigorously, controlling the number of attempts and providing clear progressions for the group; alternatively, you might encourage each athlete to work at his or her own pace and learn through trial and error.

Decision 4

You might then decide to focus on each performer and provide feedback through praise and encouragement; alternatively you might choose to focus on the errors and offer critical but constructive feedback after each attempt; or you might simply stay silent, observe and then ask questions.

Throughout each coaching session you are making decisions. Your perception of each situation along with the interaction of your goals, philosophy, knowledge, skills and experience will influence your decisions and behaviour, and the quality and effectiveness of each coaching intervention.

The Tennis Coach

Long-term goals

Player – to become a county tennis player.

Coach – to achieve the player's goal and ultimately increase Joe's independence and ability to analyse his own performance.

Session goal

Improve the consistency of Joe's service action to achieve a 60% success rate with his first serve.

Coach's philosophy

To facilitate each individual's development – physically, technically, tactically, mentally and socially – through tennis. It is based on the belief that people learn best through personal experience and the coach's role is to provide stimulating and challenging experiences to help individuals achieve their goals.

Situation

It is three quarters of the way through the coaching session. Joe cannot grasp the idea that the ball's position in the toss-up is vital to developing consistent and successful first serves.

Coach's options

Demonstrations, positive and reinforcing verbal feedback, video feedback, reflective questions, leave it for Joe to work out for himself, show the frustration that currently exists in the hope this will stir Joe into action.

Decisions

If the coach believes in and lives by his goals and philosophy, the decision he makes next should be in accord with them. The coach may try to vary the practice to improve Joe's ball toss (ie toss-up actions, feet or court positions); he may devise a ball tossing exercise with balls of different weights and sizes to improve Joe's sensitivity and coordination; he may video Joe's action and encourage Joe to analyse and discuss his findings; he may adopt a different perspective, look at the situation in a different way and re-evaluate his approach; and he may decide that it is an appropriate place to stop the session and return when they have both had a chance to rest and reflect on the progress.

This example shows that the coach has several options available to help Joe. The decision he makes will be influenced by the interaction of all the key factors – goals, philosophy, knowledge, skill, experience, emotions and the situation. Coaches who are aware of these factors can make informed and effective decisions for all concerned. They can also recognise their limitations and through self-analysis can identify ways to improve their effectiveness.

The next activity will help you analyse your current coaching tasks, decisions and behaviour. You can then gauge your effectiveness and, if appropriate, identify areas to improve.

ACTIVITY 4

1 Consider the coaching tasks you regularly undertake – it may help to think back over the last week or month. List them under the appropriate heading:

Designing and Managing the Programme or Activities	Guiding the Performers in Training	Advising the Performers in Competitive Situations	Providing other Support or Advice to the Performers

2 Select three tasks involved in guiding the performer in training and try to list the behaviours you typically employ – an example has been given to help you:

	Specific Task	Behaviours
eg	Provide feedback at the end of the session	• Ask the performers how they felt the session went and if they achieved their goals • Discuss their feelings • Give feedback on what went well • Give feedback on what did not go well • Discuss goals for next session • Agree on work before next session • Speak to individuals as necessary
1		
2		
3		

To improve *how* you coach, you need to analyse your behaviour and the reasons for your behaviour. Review these against what you already know about effective coaching and how you believe a quality coach should act. This analysis will help you decide what you would like to improve or change. Changing behaviour is usually neither quick nor easy but is essential in your journey towards your coaching excellence – at whatever level you wish to operate.

Coaching involves a range of complex tasks. How accurately can you describe how you coach? How well can you explain why you behave the way you do? How much does it vary from situation to situation? Reflect on the following questions:

- Are your instructions always helpful? When are they helpful and when are they less useful?

- Are your demonstrations and explanations always clear? When and why do you use them?

- Do you offer more praise than criticism? When? Why?

- Do you talk more than you ask or listen? When? Why?

- Does your non-verbal behaviour (ie gestures, facial expressions, posture, voice tone, appearance) always match your words? When might there be a mismatch? Why does this happen?

- Are your practices generally effective? When are they ineffective? How do you know?

- Do your performers gain sufficient and appropriate feedback to enable them to improve? How do you know? When and why do you give it?

- Do you always need to give feedback?

- How much should you give? How often?

- What factors influence the information you give? How should you give the information?

Remember your goals and those of your performers determine the overall direction of your coaching; your choice of action is influenced by the situation, your knowledge, skill and experience; and your behaviour is influenced by your philosophy (or underlying beliefs) and current emotional state.

ACTIVITY 5

Reflect on your coaching in different situations (ie outside the immediate coaching environment, in training, at competitions). Consider for example:

- how you interact socially with your athletes in and outside the coaching environment
- how you manage practices
- how you give feedback (eg type, frequency)
- your ability to analyse and seek solutions to problems
- your behaviour before, during and after competitions
- your planning and organisational skills
- your ability to action plan and goal set with athletes.

Choose one situation in which you believe you are generally successful at executing the necessary tasks and reflect on what you do, why it seems to work, when and how you do it:

Successful situation or context

Tasks	Typical Behaviours	Why Used	Why Successful

Choose one situation in which you believe you are generally less or unsuccessful at executing the necessary tasks and reflect on what you do, why it seems to be less effective, when and how you do it:

Unsuccessful situation or context

Tasks	Typical Behaviours	Why Used	Why Successful

Inevitably if you want to increase your coaching effectiveness, modify your approach or develop your skills, you first need to have a clear picture of your current thinking and behaviour. Secondly you need a clear vision of the sort of coach you want to become which will highlight the areas where you may wish to change. Several ways exist in which you can do this and the following chapters will encourage you to try each of them.

CHAPTER FIVE:
Critical Analysis and Self-reflection

Everyone engages in a certain amount of reflection. From time to time, you will think back over a particular event (eg an interview, a competition, a road traffic incident, an argument), review what happened and what you did, assess what you might have done differently or better, and perhaps determine what you might do in that situation in the future.

Maybe you do this after coaching or training sessions but probably you do not do this either consistently or systematically. You may do it more frequently when things do not go well, when you are approaching an important event such as a major competition or if you are being assessed as part of a coaching qualification[1]. In this context therefore, self-reflection simply means analysing your coaching, thinking about it and deciding how you might make it better.

To increase your coaching effectiveness, at whatever level you operate, you should develop your ability to reflect and incorporate it systematically and regularly into your coaching. This process (see Figure 4) involves the following:

- Critical evaluation by yourself and/or others to assess what happened.

- Critical analysis, to determine the effectiveness of your decisions and actions – what went well, what could have been better, what you might have done differently, the extent to which you achieved your goals and the athletes achieved theirs. This may involve comparison with what you usually do, what others you admire do, what your sport or coach educators advocate, what you believe you should do.

- Identifying improvements you want to make – these may be subtle changes that can be tried in the near future or longer term changes requiring more significant modifications which might involve gaining further knowledge, developing particular skills, extending your experience or reviewing your coaching goals and philosophy.

- Goal-setting and action planning to achieve these improvements.

- Implementing your plans.

- Reviewing and evaluating your progress.

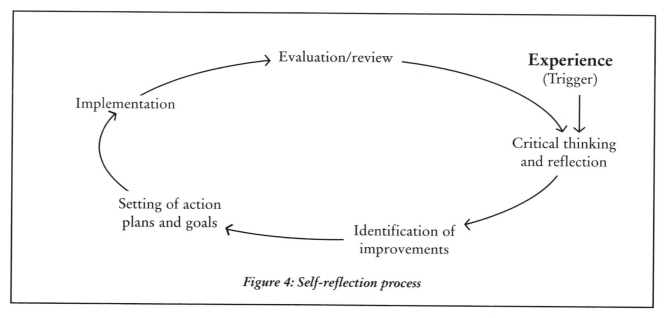

Figure 4: Self-reflection process

1 This is increasingly likely with competence-based assessment now being used in most coach education courses and qualifications. Self-evaluation and reflection are central to competence-based training and assessment.

All self-reflection requires a catalyst to trigger the process. This is usually a coaching experience but it can be prompted more frequently through the use of tools such as a coaching diary or a video clip, or with the help of a mentor coach, one of your performers or even an observant friend. These are considered in greater detail in Chapter Six (page 21).

The process of self-reflection involves:

- describing the situation and experience in a non-evaluative way first – this helps to reduce the subjectivity of your reflections

- examining and reflecting on what went well and on what was effective in that experience before focusing on things that went less well or poorly – this may require asking yourself several questions (see Appendix, page 42)

- searching for explanations which may require more self-questioning and a willingness to keep an open mind; you may need to listen to more than one point of view and be prepared to challenge your beliefs

- working through different ideas, thinking laterally and creatively to solve problems and making sense out of pieces of information

- being willing to change, work through fears or uncertainties and perhaps taking appropriate risks.

This process of self-reflection is valuable both during and after any coaching task or session. Following a session, for example, you can reflect on the extent to which you achieved your goals – both for your performers and for your coaching. This presupposes you have already developed sufficient self-awareness and motivation to work on improving your competence and effectiveness as a coach by setting yourself specific goals. You can also use reflection during your coaching sessions – look at the example in the panel on the next page.

The Reflective Tennis Coach

Goal

To increase enjoyment and competition in game play by improving service consistency (ball in court 75% of the time).

Task

Coach demonstrating the toss-up in tennis serve (but not hitting the ball) to a group of players struggling with inconsistent service actions due to irregular ball tosses.

Observations

The demonstration did not seem to be very effective as there was no consistent improvement in arm or hand action on resumption of service drill.

Critical thinking and self-reflection

Was a demonstration the best solution to achieve the goal in this situation? Could I have achieved the goal a different way? Who should have done the demonstration – me or one of the players? Was the demonstration effective? How did I position the players? Could they see clearly? How did I draw their attention to the key elements of the task – the arm/hand position, the height of release, the position of the ball in relation to the body?

How responsive were they? Did they have sufficient experience of the technique to be able to use the information in the demonstration? Did they see the correct action enough times to grasp the key points? How did I check their understanding? What impact did it have on their subsequent practice? Did I involve the players sufficiently in the evaluation process?

On reflection, a demonstration by me might not have been the best option. I might have had a better response by choosing one or two players to demonstrate their toss first and then helping the group to identify the key points. My demonstration might then have been more effective and the players might have felt more involved. When I gave the demonstration, I am not convinced they could all see what I was doing and perhaps did not see the correct action a sufficient number of times. They seemed distracted by where the ball landed rather than focusing on the position of the arm and hand at and after release and then the height of the ball above the hand. Perhaps I did not draw their attention strongly enough to the cues on which I wanted them to focus. They did not improve consistently when they returned to practise.

Specific improvements

1 Stop to consider other ways of achieving my goal.

2 If a demonstration seems the best option, consider using a player rather than myself to demonstrate the action.

3 Take care to position the group so all can see and hear clearly – check they can.

4 Provide clear instructions about what to observe (cues) before starting the demonstration.

5 Repeat the demonstration several times, each time check what they saw and re-emphasise the key points as necessary.

6 Check their understanding.

Action plans and goals

Make a note on next and subsequent session plans whenever using demonstration to stop and check it is the best option and who should give it. Watch for positioning, clarify coaching points and repeat the action three or more times. Question the players to check they have grasped the key coaching points. Note the effectiveness of each demonstration at the end of every session.

Evaluation and review

Review progress at the end of the month. Possibly seek advice from another coach.

ACTIVITY 6

Think back to your last coaching session, identify one task that worked well. Use the self-reflection process to analyse why things worked and how you might learn from that experience.

NB You can learn effectively from positive experiences, not just from things that did not work out well:

Task	Context
Critical thinking and self-reflection	
Identification of improvements	
Action plans and goals	
Evaluation and review	

Think back to your last coaching session, identify one task that did not work so well and use the self-reflection process to analyse why things did not work, what improvements might be made and how:

Task	Context
Critical thinking and self-reflection	
Identification of improvements	
Action plans and goals	
Evaluation and review	

CHAPTER SIX:
Ways to Enhance Self-reflection and Critical Analysis

Self-reflection encourages you to examine your perceptions, decisions and subsequent actions to see if more effective ways exist of helping your performers improve technically, tactically, physically, emotionally or socially. You can enhance your self-reflection, awareness and critical thinking by using tools and/or other people to help you analyse and reflect objectively and thoroughly.

Some tools can be a very valuable aid to self-analysis – they can be more lasting and accurate than your memory. They can also help you engage in ongoing learning and self-development. You can use:

- a diary to record your perceptions and reflections following each coaching intervention – any format from open ended text to a more structured check-list

- a video recording and subsequent analysis to evaluate your coaching performance directly

- an external person – a peer coach, mentor, performer or even simply an observer – to gain a different and perhaps more objective and expert view.

Each method has different benefits and you may find some work better for you than others. First you need to experience each one and assess its potential value for you, your coaching and your performers.

- Do not emulate the coaching style of others just because they have been successful.

- Find a coaching style that suits your personality and brings the best out of you. (Bloom, 1996[1])

---

1   Extract taken from Salmela, JH (1996) **Great job coach.** Potentium, Ottawa. ISBN 0 9680935 0 7.

Using a Diary or Coaches' Log

Diaries come in all shapes and sizes and fulfil many roles. Most people have used a diary in some way – to make appointments, remember birthdays, record personal thoughts, log training sessions. People use diaries most frequently to aid their memory or planning. Diaries can be powerful tools in aiding self-reflection, planning and in monitoring progress. In this way, they can help you to improve your coaching effectiveness.

To assess how useful a diary may be, you first need to try using it for a week or more. You could start using a diary for self-reflection after a coaching or training session. You may wish to focus on just one aspect of your coaching – for example your session planning, organisation, management or your communication, teaching/coaching. Initially, you should structure the information you put into your diary. This can then prompt you to include appropriate information in future entries. The following pages (from which you may wish to make photocopies) provide structured formats which may help you record what happened, your evaluation, your self-reflections and ultimately your strategies for change. Alternatively, and certainly in time, you may wish to adapt these formats or use an unstructured format. You should find the list of questions in the Appendix (page 42) useful, irrespective of how you choose to record your analysis and reflections.

These guidelines can help you achieve the greatest benefit from a coaching diary:

- Write your diary entry soon after the coaching intervention (session, competition, interview, planning), while your thoughts are fresh.

- Write in whatever format suits you – note form, diagram, flow chart, on computer.

- Always write down what happened first – describe the situation, your perceptions, decisions and behaviour before evaluating what was good and not so good.

- You may wish to focus on what went well first – the best insights are often gained from positive experiences. Having described what went well and in what way your performance was effective, then try to think why, reflect on what you were thinking and feeling.

- Describe what did not go well (eg a situation, a particular practice) and where you feel you could improve. Work out why it did not go well, what you were thinking and feeling at the time.

- Next identify ways in which you could improve – perhaps a different approach, more detailed planning, more or less intervention. If you cannot readily find a way forward, go back to your coaching goals, and reflect on your philosophy and the goals of your performers. Jot down a list of ideas – just as they come into your head without stopping to evaluate them. Now review them and list them in an order which most benefits your performers.

- Be patient with yourself, be willing to consider other perceptions and keep your coaching goals and philosophy in mind.

Coaching Diary Session I

Date:

Reflection focus (if you have one):

Context/situation:

Describe the coaching session/situation:

Describe a situation in which you were effective and explain why:

Describe a situation in which you were ineffective and explain why:

List the improvements you wish to make, suggest a plan of action and identify when you will implement your plan[1]:

Note any other observation:

1 At this stage, you may not feel ready to do this. Don't worry, you can come back to this exercise a little later.

Subsequent Coaching Diary Entries

Date:

Reflection focus (if you have one):

Context/situation:

Describe the coaching session/situation:

Describe a situation in which you were effective and explain why. Use the prompt questions in the Appendix (page 42) to help you:

Describe a situation in which you were ineffective and explain why. Use the prompt questions in the Appendix (page 42) to help you:

List the improvements you wish to make and suggest a plan of action and when you will implement them[1]:

Note any changes you made based on a previous diary entry and any further action you may now want to take:

Note any other observation:

---

1   At this stage, you may not feel ready to do this. Don't worry, you can come back to this exercise a little later.

Using a Coaching Diary

Benefits

Written record over time which can show progress.

Personal so you can be honest and record feelings, emotions and actions.

Tips

Use concise notes so it does not become time consuming.

Describe what happened first including situation, performers, session goals before starting your evaluation.

Consider the performers' responses and why they behaved the way they did.

Focus on what was good as well as what you want to improve.

Try to explain why things went well or badly.

Think about your goals, philosophy, knowledge, skills and experience and use a brainstorming session to generate many ways to improve – if there is not one clear option, then prioritise.

ACTIVITY 7

Use a coaching diary for a week and make at least six entries to see how well this tool helps you to become more critical, self-reflective and ultimately more effective in your coaching.

- How was the diary useful?

- What difficulties did you experience?

- How could you adapt the diary to make it more useful?

- Did you gain any specific insights into your coaching (or the performers) you want to address?

If you found this process worthwhile, you might consider incorporating a coaching diary regularly into your coaching to help you analyse and reflect on your effectiveness.

Effective coaches take responsibility for their effectiveness.

Using Video and Checklists

Video self-analysis provides an excellent way to assess and improve your coaching effectiveness. Turn the camera on yourself during a training session, at a competition, at a time-out, when giving an athlete feedback or in a goal-setting session. You will have an objective record of what happened which you can subsequently analyse and re-analyse in slow motion or in real time to help you examine your perceptions, thoughts, decisions and actions in relation to your goals and philosophy and your performers' responses and goals. You will see yourself as others see you and will have a complete record rather than one limited by memory and subjectivity. You can use the video clip to analyse a particular situation and your response to that situation (eg a content analysis of your communication skills, your non-verbal behaviour, your half-time talk) or to conduct a more general evaluation, perhaps using a check-list.

To assess how useful video may be to you, you first need to try using it during a coaching session or competition, or perhaps in an interview with an athlete (ensure you explain the video's purpose to the performer in advance and gain his or her permission). The following guidelines may help you to make a video recording of the relevant action that you can use for your self-analysis.

Guidelines

1   Identify someone to operate the camera and give them a tripod. Brief the operator carefully about what you want to record and encourage the use of auto-focus, exposure and balance (these are standard on most camcorders) to provide a quality recording.

2   Ensure you can pick up all sound (your voice, the performer's). A radio-microphone is ideal to pick up your voice (but not necessarily the performer's). If a radio-microphone is not possible or you want to record what each performer says, ensure the operator stays within 2–3 metres of you.

3   The positioning of the camera is crucial. Depending on the sport and what it is you want to record, you will need to decide whether or not the camera and operator need to be mobile. Think about what you need to see. Just your actions? What you say? Your interaction with the performers? Your facial expressions and gestures? The way your performers respond? The overall session?

4   Whatever you are recording, it may be a good idea to start the camera before the actual action starts – think of the important information you might obtain before the start or at the end of the session/competition.

5   Ensure you have enough film and always label and date the video at the end. You may want to go back and review it later.

Before you start to analyse the video, decide whether you will:

- do a general analysis using a checklist (an example is provided on page 28) – this may be necessary on the first video analysis you do

- focus on one aspect of your coaching (eg when and how effectively you give feedback, when and how effectively you listen, the speed and effectiveness of your group management)

- identify effective and ineffective situations and analyse them in a similar way to the method you used in the diary.

Remember to focus on the way you behave as well as what you say and why you say it. Ask yourself 'Could I have done this better?'. You may want to note particular situations or issues on the tape counter so you can find them again quickly.

Communicating	Teaching	Managing
Planning	Facilitating	Disciplining
Enquiring	Explaining	Organising
Reflecting	Informing	Gaining attention
Analysing	Questioning	Controlling
Reading	Demonstrating	Planning
Learning	Commenting	Timing
Informing	Monitoring	Transitions
Listening	Appraising	Instructing
Socialising	Criticising	Delegating
Praising	Correcting	Supervising
Friendly	Advising	Safeguarding
Questioning/asking	Challenging	Setting up drills/practices
Challenging	Feeding back	
Supporting	Observing	
Telling	Analysing	
Instructing		
Chatting		
Non-verbal cues		
Flexible		
Approachable		
Humour		
Caring		

Using Video Self-analysis

Benefits	Tips
Objective – see yourself as others see you.	Find someone to operate the camera, give them a tripod and mains supply to use. Also use the auto focus if possible and consider location carefully.
Replay facility, slow motion and freeze frame to enhance analysis.	Stay within a few metres or use a microphone to ensure all sound is recorded.
Replay as often as you like.	Start recording well before the session officially starts and continue after the finish – there are often important interactions at these times.
Can see progress and changes over time.	Focus on how you are coaching as well as what you are coaching.
	Label and store for future play.

ACTIVITY 8

Decide how you will use video to enhance your self-analysis. Will you conduct a general analysis of a whole training or coaching session? Have you already determined a specific situation (eg presenting a demonstration, giving specific feedback to one performer, before competition, at a time out) in which you want to examine your coaching more closely? Organise people to help video the selected aspect of your coaching, review the video and note down:

- in what ways the video clip was a useful record of your coaching:

- any filming difficulties you experienced:

Now analyse the clip. You may choose to do this by using an available checklist (such as the one on page 28) or you may prefer to develop your own checklist. Alternatively, you may choose to review the video, make notes and ask yourself critical and self-reflective questions about why you did what you did, the extent to which this was successful, how you might have done it better and so on. Remember a list of prompt questions is available to help you in the Appendix (page 42).

- How was the video useful?

- How was the checklist useful?

- What difficulties did you experience?

- How could you make the video/checklist more useful?

- Did you gain any specific insights into your coaching that you want to address?

If you found video self-analysis useful for reflecting on your perceptions, decisions and actions and enhancing your effectiveness, you may like to make it a regular part of your coaching. Analysing your coaching on video is an excellent way of ensuring you continue to improve your coaching. Remember effective coaches take responsibility for their effectiveness.

Using Others to Facilitate Analysis and Reflection

Involving someone else in the process of analysing your coaching can help you develop your self-analysis and critical self-reflection skills, and provide an objective viewpoint. Whether this is done with the help of a performer, a friend (a non-expert observer), a colleague or a mentor coach, it can provide a degree of objectivity. You are reflecting with another person rather than alone and in silence. The other person can serve as an observer and sounding board – listening to what you say, posing questions and if they have coaching expertise, providing constructive feedback and advice. Again it is important to focus on the *What did I do?*, *How?* and *Why?* of your coaching. The process is trying to help you analyse your coaching so you can improve its effectiveness.

> *Mentors help coaches to recognise and maximise learning opportunities.*
>
> *Galvin, B (1998)*
> *A guide to mentoring sports coaches, scUK*

Coaching provides many opportunities for learning. Throughout this resource the emphasis has been on analysing your current coaching to identify the areas where you can increase your knowledge and skill, reflect on your perceptions, behaviour, emotions and experiences, and clarify your goals and philosophy. The quote in the panel above emphasises that a mentor coach can be invaluable in helping you identify and maximise these learning opportunities in a way you might not do when working on your own.

Using Others

Benefits
Sounding board who can pose questions and provide constructive and objective feedback.

Tips
Focus on a recent training session.

Do not judge but provide information and ask questions.

You determine the focus.

Always describe your performance before you and your mentor evaluate it; this approach helps provide a balanced assessment and enables greater clarity of thinking.

Note down key points after the meeting.

ACTIVITY 9

Try to find someone who is willing to observe your coaching and act as a sounding board, an objective eye and who will ask the all-important questions to help you become a more effective coach. Ideally, this would be a mentor coach but if this is not possible at present, ask anyone you trust to fulfil this role. In the same way you briefed your video operator, you may wish to focus your observer's attention on a particular situation or a specific aspect of your coaching. You could encourage the observer to write notes, talk into a hand-held recorder or complete a checklist while observing you. Alternatively, you might ask the observer to review one of your video clips with you. Whatever your choice, set up the situation and then assess the observer's impact and contribution by noting down:

- How did the observer help you?

- What difficulties did you experience?

- How could you make the observer's contribution more useful?

- Any insights into your coaching you may wish to address:

If you found the external observer a useful stimulus for your critical thinking and self-reflection, it may be worth making a deliberate effort to discuss your coaching with other coaches regularly. Sharing observations and ideas with other coaches is one of the most powerful ways of making self-reflection and analysis a regular part of your coaching. You might even like to develop a more formal relationship with another coach and review the role of the mentor more fully. Alternatively you might establish a coaching group where you can share ideas and discuss issues regularly with other coaches.

Coaches from the same sport can help you explore the technical aspects of your coaching; coaches from other sports can help stimulate your creativity or offer alternative suggestions from different perspectives. Coaches who operate at different levels can share their experiences and knowledge to help your effectiveness. You, in turn, can offer support to other coaches in the group. Others will automatically become involved in the analytical process and will enhance their effectiveness and that of their sports performers.

CHAPTER SEVEN:
The Mentor's Role

Perhaps you are fortunate enough to find a mentor coach – a coach with perhaps more or different experiences – who is willing to help you improve your coaching. Good mentors can help you in several ways. In the first phase of analysing your coaching, they can:

- help you gain more accurate or comprehensive information about your coaching

- enhance your ability to analyse and then reflect by listening and questioning, and challenging your actions and beliefs.

At a later stage, when you have decided in what way you want to change or develop your coaching, they can also help by:

- clarifying an action plan with you (see Chapter Eight, page 34)

- providing you with a role model to extend your experience (not necessarily to copy because the way you coach should match your situation, goals, philosophy and those of your performers)

- being a resource that can direct you to up-to-date knowledge or coach education workshops

- supporting you as you implement your plan and providing you with feedback and ideas

- coaching you to help develop your coaching skills.

The **scUK** resource, *A Guide to Mentoring Sports Coaches*[1] is of value to the mentor coach and the coach being mentored. You might want to try the following process, with the help of a mentor, to help you develop your analytical and self-reflective skills.

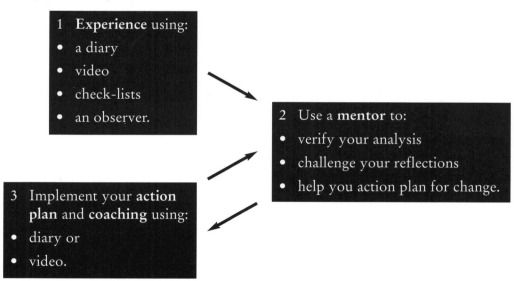

Having determined the value of videos, diaries and mentors and identified the areas in which you wish to change or develop, the next stage is to decide **how** you are going to change or develop. Essentially, you should formulate an action plan. This plan should contain specific tasks and deadlines for you to achieve your desired changes. Creating and implementing this plan is an essential part of increasing your effectiveness as a coach; it helps to guide your development, gauge your progress and motivate you along your path to excellence.

1   Available from **Coachwise 1st4sport** (tel 0113-201 5555 or visit www.1st4sport.com).

CHAPTER EIGHT:
Action Planning

Once you have tried using a coaching diary, video recordings and the help of an observer, you will begin to know what works well for you. Remember if you are to engage in constant reflection and improvement, you will need to develop your critical thinking and self-reflection skills. You cannot always rely on the eye and guidance of a mentor. However, this external perspective will be valuable from time to time. As you analyse and reflect on your coaching more frequently and systematically, you will identify aspects of your coaching you want to develop or change. You may already have begun to do this when you used the diary, video and mentor.

Once you have identified what you want to change or develop and have decided it is a practical and realistic goal, then it is time to action plan. Action planning involves identifying several steps (or goals) to help you improve your coaching effectiveness. This process is no different from the goal-setting process you would adopt with your performers, but this time it focuses on your coaching.

Having examined your strengths and weaknesses and prioritised the areas on which you want to focus, you need to clarify exactly what you want to achieve, how best you might do this and how long you will reasonably need to make this change. Look at the following example which shows how a hockey coach identified what he wanted to improve, how he set goals and the process he used to implement the plan.

Behaviour identified

Based on his reflections and substantiated by video recordings, Phil, a hockey coach, identifies a weakness in his ability to use half-time talks effectively. He has identified that although he analyses the game quite well, he tries to give too much information, often in an unstructured way and sometimes rather negatively. The result verified by some of his players, is that the team tends to feel bombarded with information, uncertain about what is required of them in the second half and consequently with reduced self-confidence in their ability to win the match.

Prioritised action/long term goal

Having identified the issues (too much unstructured and negative information), Phil decides to develop a strategy for using half-time talks effectively. His time frame is six months.

Medium-/short-term goals

Identify what key information is relevant to give to the players at half time (ie extend his knowledge).

Examine how best to structure and give feedback by analysing how more experienced coaches structure and give their half-time talks (ie develop his skill).

Reflect why he gives the information negatively (ie reflect on his experience).

Process

- Know his players better to understand what is important to them and provide specific and relevant feedback to each player.

- Ask permission from the senior coach to video his half-time talks over the next month, analyse these to examine the content of the intervention, the amount of information offered and the way it is given (gain from another coach's experience).

- Contact England Hockey and **scUK** to request any articles or guidance each may have on this topic (further knowledge).

- Attend a communication workshop to help him examine his communication skills (skill development).

- Analyse his thoughts and feelings at half-time.

- Examine why he feels the way he does.

- Identify other ways of looking at the coaching situation.

- Consider the manner in which he would like to give the feedback (and simultaneously examine his philosophy).

- Adopt and implement the approach in future games.

Following this action, Phil formulates his strategy and can therefore set his next medium- and short-term goals.

Medium-/short-term goals

Summarise the team's main strengths in one sentence; similarly the team's major weaknesses.

Provide no more than three pieces of information for the players to go out on the pitch and implement; given in a positive and clear manner.

Offer individual comment over and above this if absolutely essential.

Process

- To design a simple chart with space only for the points to be included.

- During the last five minutes of play, he will check out his match analysis with the statistics and write down the main strength and weakness on the chart. He will then identify up to three (preferably one or two) key pointers for the remainder of the match. Essential individual comments will also be committed to the chart.

- He will take the chart onto the pitch, wait for the players to get their drinking bottles and then restrict himself only to the information on the chart. He will use video to check on the content and delivery and set further short-term goals for each match.

Half-time Talk Chart

Match against:

Date: Venue:

Strengths: Weaknesses:

Action Point 1:

Action Point 2:

Action Point 3:

Player: Comment:

In this example, Phil identified a realistic example in which he was being ineffective. He also identified the fundamental issues in the situation he wished to address. He then increased his knowledge of the important issues for each player (this process took two months to help each player open up and have the confidence to examine his feelings); increased his coaching skill by analysing another coach, reading relevant articles and attending a workshop; and reflected on his experience to gauge how he was giving the feedback, and how he would like to give it. He then devised an action plan to increase and monitor his effectiveness.

ACTIVITY 10

From the analyses and reflections you have already undertaken, now construct your action plan.

Remember to base all your goals on the SMART principle:

S pecific – make them as precise as possible, woolly goals are of no use

M easurable – ensure they are quantifiable so you can monitor progress

A cceptable – commit to the goals, want to make that improvement

R ealistic – make sure the goals are practical

T ime-phased – put a time-scale on each goal

Personal action plan to improve my coaching

- Situation identified:

- Prioritised action or long-term goal:

Medium-/Short-term Goals	Process

You may find it difficult to think of ways to action plan to change your coaching. Sometimes it helps just to do a brainstorming session and jot down all the possible – even crazy – ways that come into your head. Look at them and start to whittle them down to one or more that seem to suit you and your situation. You may find it helpful to consider the routes outlined in the following table.

Would I Move Closer to my Goal if:			
I had more or new knowledge?	I had more or different experience?	I had new or more developed skills?	my actions matched my beliefs more closely?
↓	↓	↓	↓
Consider tracking down books, articles from your NGB or scUK[1]	Look for a coach who seems to be effective in the area – from your own or even a different sport[2]	Find a workshop or study resource which specifies help with the skill you are seeking to develop – try your NGB and scUK[3]	If you want to understand better why you behave the way you do, you may want to engage in self-reflection – ask more questions of yourself – why you act the way you do?

Having established your action plan, the final stage in the process is to implement your plan. As you do, keep in mind your goals and philosophy as they will direct and guide your actions. As an analytical and reflective coach, you should start to see the benefits of your analyses in your effectiveness and that of your performers. The process, however, does not stop when you implement your plan; it is cyclic so you continually analyse your practice; reflect on your perceptions, decisions and actions; identify areas for development; plan the appropriate changes; and implement the changes (see Figure 3 on page 5). Using this process will help to refine your practice and increase your effectiveness and also that of your performers.

---

1 See page 39.

2 Obtain a copy of **scUK's** *Guide to Mentoring Sports Coaches* from **Coachwise 1st4sport** (tel 0113-201 5555 or visit www.1st4sport.com).

3 See page 40.

CHAPTER NINE:
What Next?

If you have reached this page in the resource, you have successfully taken the first step in increasing your coaching effectiveness by increasing your knowledge. The next step is to increase your skill of self-analysis by implementing the information in this pack:

- Visualise the ideal coach and identify their main qualities.

- Examine your beliefs and values and compare them with your ideal coach's beliefs and values.

- Analyse your current behaviour, decisions, thoughts and perceptions through the use of video, a diary or a mentor coach.

- Compare your analysis with how you envisage your ideal coach would behave and think.

- Determine your personal coaching goals (they should be similar to your ideal coach).

- Plan specific tasks and dates to achieve your goals.

- Implement your plan to increase your coaching effectiveness.

As you go through this process, reflect on your experiences and strive towards emulating your ideal coach and increasing your effectiveness. The benefits you will receive include:

- a clear sense of direction

- a set of guidelines for good practice (ie your philosophy, values and beliefs)

- increased knowledge, skill and experiences.

Your performers should benefit from having a more effective coach who can help them develop socially and emotionally, as well as physically, mentally, technically and tactically. Remember *effective coaches take responsibility for their effectiveness* so start analysing your coaching and become a more effective coach.

The following will complement the information provided in this resource:

Galvin, B (1998) **A guide to mentoring sports coaches.** Leeds, **Coachwise Business Solutions/**The National Coaching Foundation. ISBN 1 902523 03 2[1]

Hagger, M and Earle, C (2003) **Coaching young performers (2nd edition).** Leeds, **Coachwise Business Solutions/**The National Coaching Foundation. ISBN 1 902523 56 3[2]

Layton, R (1998) **Coaching better: becoming a more effective coach.** Australian Coaching Council

Hackett, P and Hackett, S (2005) **Creating a Safe Coaching Environment.** Leeds, **Coachwise Business Solutions/**The National Coaching Foundation. ISBN 1 902523 71 1[3]

Salmela, JH (1996) **Great job coach.** Potentium, Ottawa. ISBN 0 9680935 0 7

1, 2 and 3   Available from **Coachwise 1st4sport** (tel 0113-201 5555 or visit www.1st4sport.com).

To continue to update and develop your coaching knowledge and skills, you are advised to take note of the resources recommended throughout this resource. These will help to extend your knowledge further on specific topics and improve your coaching.

Recommended **scUK** workshops and resources (complimentary with the corresponding workshop) include:

scUK Workshop	Resource
A Guide to Mentoring Sports Coaches	A Guide to Mentoring Sports Coaches
Analysing Your Coaching	Analysing Your Coaching
Coaching and the Law	–
Coaching Children and Young People	Coaching Young Performers
Coaching Disabled Performers	Coaching Disabled Performers
Coaching Methods and Communication	The Successful Coach
Creating a Safe Coaching Environment	Creating a Safe Coaching Environment
Equity in Your Coaching	Equity in Your Coaching
Field Based Fitness Testing	A Guide to Field Based Fitness Testing
Fitness and Training	Physiology and Performance
Fuelling Performers	Fuelling Performers
Goal-setting and Planning	Planning Coaching Programmes
Good Practice and Child Protection	Protecting Children
Imagery Training	Imagery Training
Improving Practices and Skill	Improving Practices and Skill
Injury Prevention and Management	Sports Injury
Motivation and Mental Toughness	Motivation and Mental Toughness
Observation, Analysis and Video	Observation, Analysis and Video
Performance Profiling	Performance Profiling
The Responsible Sports Coach	–
Understanding Eating Disorders	–

All **scUK** resources are available from:

Coachwise 1st4sport
Coachwise Ltd
Chelsea Close
Off Amberley Road
Armley
Leeds LS12 4HP
Tel: 0113-201 5555
Fax: 0113-231 9606
E-mail: enquiries@1st4sport.com
Website: www.1st4sport.com

scUK also produces a technical journal – *Faster, Higher, Stronger (FHS)* and an information update service for coaches (**sports coach update**). Details of these services are available from:

sports coach UK
114 Cardigan Road
Headingley
Leeds LS6 3BJ
Tel: 0113-274 4802
Fax: 0113-275 5019
E-mail: coaching@sportscoachuk.org
Website: www.sportscoachuk.org

sports coach UK work closely with sports governing bodies and other partners to provide a comprehensive service for coaches throughout the UK. This includes an extensive programme of workshops, which have proved valuable to coaches from all types of sport and every level of experience.

For further details of **scUK** workshops in your area, contact the **scUK**
Business Support Centre (BSC).

sports coach UK Business Support Centre
Sports Development Centre
Loughborough University
Loughborough
Leicestershire LE11 3TU
Tel: 01509-226130
Fax: 01509-226134
Email: bsc@sportscoachuk.org

APPENDIX:
Questions to Prompt Self-reflection

General Reflective Questions

What was I trying to achieve?

Why did I intervene as I did?

What were the consequences of my actions (for me, my performers, others)?

How did I feel about this experience when it was happening?

How did the performers feel about it?

How do I know how they felt about it?

What internal factors influenced my decisions?

What external factors influenced my decisions?

What knowledge should have influenced my decisions?

Could I have dealt better with the situation?

What other choices did I have?

What would be the consequences of these choices?

How do I feel now about the experience?

What have I learnt – about coaching in general, my ethical stance, about myself, about my performers?

How have I made sense of this experience?

How will it affect my future practice?

Specific Questions to Prompt Critical Thinking and Self-reflection[1]

Planning, organising and managing sessions

How do I plan my coaching sessions?

Do my sessions run smoothly? Do they begin and end on time? Are the transitions between activities quick, smooth and efficient? Do I use standard ways to do things so performers respond quickly?

How do I gain my performers' attention? Does it work? Do I talk over the top of them until they attend? Do I wait until they are quiet and watching? Do I need to discipline my performers? How do I deal with discipline problems? Can I discipline a performer without putting them down? Do I do it publicly or wait to speak to them after the session? Why would I do it?

Do I do all the organising or do I delegate tasks to others? Who is responsible for setting up and putting away equipment? Do performers automatically start warming-up when they arrive or do they wait for my instruction?

---

1   Many of these prompt questions have been based on ideas from the Australian Coaching Council's Level 1 study pack *Coaching Better: becoming a more effective coach.*

What impression do I give? What kind of role model am I? Am I active and enthusiastic, punctual, appropriately dressed – tidy and smart? Am I loud and bossy? Am I gentle but assertive? Am I too formal or too informal? How do my performers respond to me?

Am I sufficiently aware of safety considerations before, during and after the session? Do I check the facilities beforehand? Can I gain first aid when I need it? Can I always gain access to a phone?

Communication

How do I communicate with my performers? Do I rely on questions? Do I use plenty of humour or sarcasm? Do I laugh with my performers or at them? Are my instructions clear and helpful? How do I know my performers have understood? Do I talk more than I ask or listen? Do I encourage performers to contribute? How well do I listen? Can I counsel performers who come to me with problems effectively? How well do I know each performer – home life as well as sporting life?

What verbal and non-verbal signals do I give people? Do I have any potentially annoying or distracting non-verbal behaviours? Does my non-verbal behaviour (gestures, facial expressions, posture, voice tone, appearance) reflect my words? Am I approachable? Am I courteous and do I show my performers respect?

Am I fairly formal or quite relaxed in my general approach? How would I describe my communication style? Does my behaviour reflect my philosophy and beliefs? Can I adapt my communication style to suit each situation and performer?

Are my demonstrations and explanations clear? Do I offer more praise than criticism? Do my performers gain sufficient and appropriate feedback to enable them to improve?

Teaching

Do I plan the way I will teach a technique or tactic? Does it follow a pattern? Do I provide the right amount of information, too little or too much? Do I overload the performers with information? Do I focus on just one or two coaching points?

Are my demonstrations clear and effective? Are they visible to all my performers? Do I do all the demonstrations or do I use my performers whenever possible? Do I point out where they should focus their attention? How do I know these points are the most appropriate?

Are my practices effective? Do I give the performers time to practise before I intervene and provide additional instructions or feedback? Do I give them time to process their intrinsic feedback before I provide additional information? Are my practices challenging to all – even the most talented? Do I focus on the more talented and ignore the less able? Does every performer gain personal feedback every session? How do I monitor drills to check they are effective? How do my performers respond to my practices and feedback?

Do I use questioning as a coaching method? What kind of questions do I ask? Are they knowledge-based (How should you stop the ball?)? Are they more demanding – perhaps asking why or requiring a decision (eg what could you do in this situation? How will you decide which option to take?)?

RESTON COLLEGE
WILLIAM TUSON LIBRARY